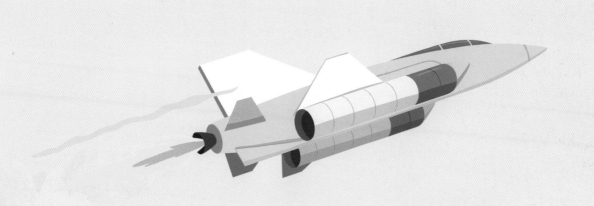

Author:

Ian Graham earned a diploma in applied physics at City University, London. He then earned a graduate degree in journalism. Since becoming a freelance author and journalist, he has written more than 250 children's nonfiction books.

Series creator:

David Salariya was born in Dundee, Scotland. He has illustrated a wide range of books and has created and designed many new series for publishers in the UK and overseas. David established The Salariya Book Company in 1989. He lives in Brighton, England, with his wife, illustrator Shirley Willis, and their son, Jonathan.

Artists:

Christos Skaltsas, Bryan Beach, Jared Green, Sam Bridges, and Shutterstock.

Editor:

Nick Pierce

© The Salariya Book Company Ltd MMXIX
No part of this publication may be reproduced in whole or in part, or stored in a retrieval system, or transmitted in any form or by any means, electronic, mechanical, photocopying, recording, or otherwise, without written permission of the publisher. For information regarding permission, write to the copyright holder.

Published in Great Britain in 2019 by
The Salariya Book Company Ltd
25 Marlborough Place, Brighton BN1 1UB

Library of Congress Cataloging-in-Publication Data

Names: Graham, Ian, 1953- author. | Skaltsas, Christos, illustrator. | Beach, Bryan, illustrator.
Title: The science of flight : the air-amazing truth about planes and helicopters / written by Ian Graham ; [artists, Christos Skaltsas, Bryan Beach].
Description: New York, NY : Franklin Watts, an imprint of Scholastic Inc., 2019. | Series: The science of... | Includes index.
Identifiers: LCCN 2018031800| ISBN 9780531131954 (library binding) | ISBN 9780531133958 (pbk.)
Subjects: LCSH: Aeronautics--Juvenile literature. | Airplanes--Design and construction--Juvenile literature. | Helicopters--Design and construction--Juvenile literature. | Flying-machines--Juvenile literature.
Classification: LCC TL547 .G765 2019 | DDC 629.13--dc23

All rights reserved.
Published in 2019 in the United States
by Franklin Watts
An imprint of Scholastic Inc.

Printed and bound in China.
Printed on paper from sustainable sources.
1 2 3 4 5 6 7 8 9 10 R 28 27 26 25 24 23 22 21 20 19

PAPER FROM
SUSTAINABLE
FORESTS

The Science of Flight

Flight

The Air-mazing Truth About Planes and Helicopters

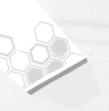

written by
Ian Graham

Franklin Watts®
An Imprint of Scholastic Inc.

Contents

Introduction

For most of human history, people gazed at birds in awe of their mastery of flight. When people tried to copy the birds by strapping on wings and flapping their arms, they couldn't get off the ground. In England in 1853, Sir George Cayley built a glider that managed to make a short hop into the air. In Germany in the 1890s, Otto Lilienthal made short flights using his own gliders.

The secret of flight was finally cracked in the early 1900s by the American brothers Wilbur and Orville Wright. First, they built kites and gliders, and learned how to control them in the air. Then they added power—an engine driving two propellers.

On December 17, 1903, Orville Wright made the first powered, controlled flight in a heavier-than-air flying machine, an airplane called the *Flyer*. Every airplane today can trace its history back to the Wright brothers' *Flyer*, but things have come a long way since then.

The Forces of Flight

Smooth

Anything that sticks out of a plane causes more drag and slows it down. The plane's engines have to burn more fuel to overcome any extra drag. Planes are made as smooth as possible so that air can flow over them easily, with the least possible drag.

The same four forces act on all powered aircraft. They are lift, weight, thrust, and drag. Lift produced by wings pushes a plane upward, while weight pulls it down. Thrust produced by engines moves it forward, while drag slows it down. Drag is a force caused by air pushing against a moving plane. Weight, produced by the action of gravity on an aircraft, is present all the time, but the other three forces of flight are created by the aircraft and its motion. Designers try to make the most of lift and thrust by cutting an aircraft's weight and drag.

Lift and drag always go together in airplanes. When a wing moves through the air faster it produces more lift, which also creates more drag.

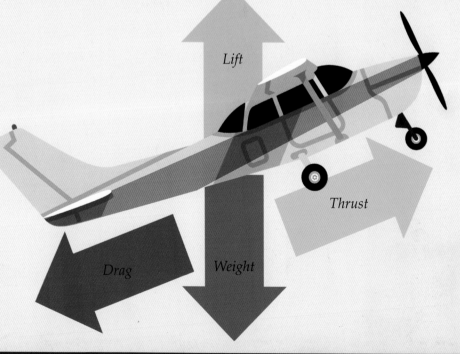

Lift

Thrust

Drag

Weight

Slimming Down

Have you ever wondered why planes have a long, slim body, and aren't box-shaped? Planes are made with a long, tube-shaped body so that they can move through the air more easily. A box-shaped aircraft would create too much drag.

It'll never fly, it's too short!

Fascinating Fact

An airliner's takeoff speed is calculated for each flight. It depends on the aircraft's weight, how many passengers and how much fuel it's carrying, the air temperature, and the height of the airport above sea level.

Keep It Light

To save weight, most planes are made of lightweight materials such as aluminum and plastic. Under a plane's smooth skin, there is a frame that combines light weight with great strength.

An airliner has to reach a speed of about 160 miles per hour (260 kilometers per hour) before its wings produce enough lift for the plane to take off.

7

The Magic of Wings

A Clever Shape

A wing's shape deflects air downward. The air pushes back, creating an upward force of lift. Air pressure above the wing falls, and pressure below it rises, creating more lift. Tilting a wing magnifies this effect and creates even more lift.

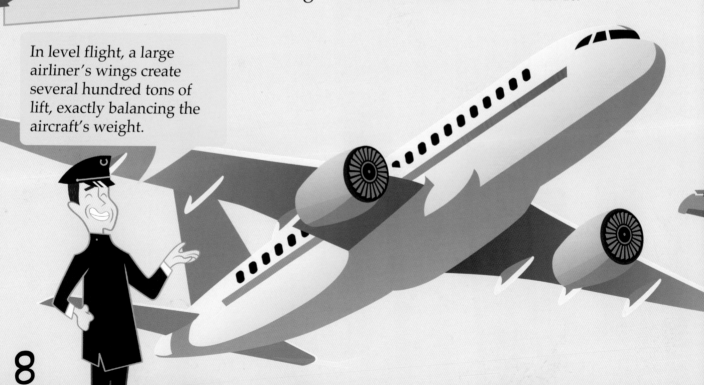

Wings do something amazing. When they move through air, they create the upward force of lift that enables heavier-than-air planes to fly. A wing's secret is its special shape, called an airfoil. It works by changing the direction of the air flowing around it. A wing has to keep moving to create lift. As soon as it stops, there is no lift. And if a wing slows down too much or tilts up at the front too much, it can suddenly lose all lift. This sudden loss of lift is called stalling. Pilots are trained to avoid it.

In level flight, a large airliner's wings create several hundred tons of lift, exactly balancing the aircraft's weight.

Planes designed for use on warships called aircraft carriers often have folding wings so that they take up less space on the ship.

Dangerous Ice!

If water freezes on a wing, it can interfere with the wing's smooth airfoil shape. An ice-covered wing produces less lift, which can be dangerous.

In freezing weather, airliners are often sprayed with an antifreeze chemical that keeps ice from forming or melts ice on the wings and tail.

Slats and Flaps

At takeoff and landing, a plane flies slowly and its wings create less lift. To make more lift for flying safely at lower speeds, planes make their wings bigger. Panels called slats slide out in front of each wing, and panels called flaps slide out at the back.

Slats

Flaps

Fascinating Fact

Giant airliners need huge wings to lift their massive weight into the air. The Airbus A380's wings cover an area big enough to hold 70 cars.

The Power to Fly

The power to fly is provided by an aircraft's engine. The engine works by burning fuel. An engine that burns fuel inside it is called an internal combustion engine. Burning is a chemical reaction between the fuel and oxygen in the air. The chemical reaction gives out energy in the form of heat. Heating the gases inside the engine makes them expand very quickly. The force of the expanding gas can then turn a propeller or form the powerful jet of gas produced by a jet engine.

Piston Engines

The smallest planes are powered by engines that work like car engines. Fuel burns in a series of explosions inside the engine, making pistons move back and forth, turning a shaft that spins a propeller. The spinning propeller pushes air backward to make the plane move forward.

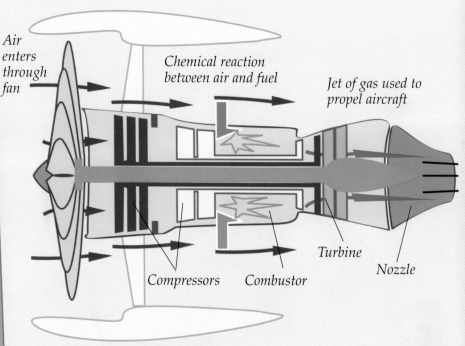

Air enters through fan

Chemical reaction between air and fuel

Jet of gas used to propel aircraft

Compressors   Combustor   Turbine   Nozzle

Jet Power

Most of the biggest and fastest planes are powered by jet engines. A large jet engine accelerates the air flowing through it to a speed of about 1,300 miles per hour (2,100 kph). Because of this, the jet blast behind a plane can pose a hazard to nearby vehicles.

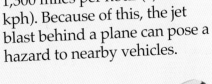

That's a powerful engine!

If an airliner's engines stop working, it doesn't fall out of the sky. A large airliner can glide without engine power for about 100 miles (160 km).

Can You Believe It?

Fuel burning inside a jet engine can reach a temperature of 3,500 degrees Fahrenheit (2,000 degrees Celsius). Parts of the engine begin to melt at 2,372°F (1,300°C), so jet engines need sophisticated cooling systems to stop them from melting!

Fan Jets

Most large airliners use a type of jet engine called a turbofan. The jet engine spins a big fan like a propeller with dozens of blades. The fan, at the front of the engine, produces most of the engine's power and thrust.

It's huge!

Delta Wing

A triangular wing called a delta wing is a very good shape for supersonic flight. Planes with delta wings look a little like paper darts.

Faster Than Sound

As faster and faster aircraft were built, their top speed began to get close to the speed of sound. But pilots found that their planes suffered a sudden increase in drag as they neared the speed of sound. The planes often became difficult to control. The speed of sound seemed to be a wall that couldn't be crossed. It became known as the sound barrier. But eventually designers learned how to make planes that could fly faster than sound. They are supersonic. Speeds faster than five times the speed of sound are hypersonic.

The speed of sound in air depends on how warm or cold the air is. Whatever the actual speed is, the speed of sound is also called mach 1.

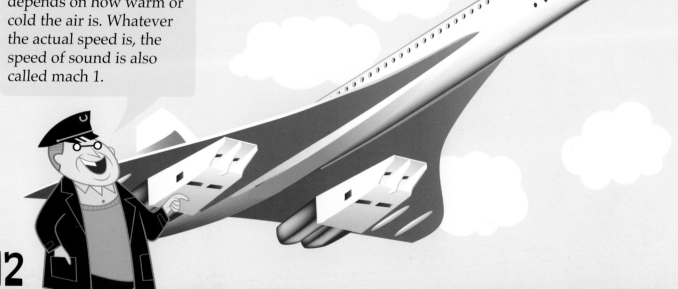

Sonic Boom

When a plane flies faster than sound, it squishes the air in front of it. This squished air is called a shock wave. The shock wave spreads out from the aircraft, and if it sweeps over people on the ground, they hear it as a loud bang called a sonic boom.

Even Faster

An experimental hypersonic aircraft called the X-51A reached speeds over five times the speed of sound during a test flight in 2013. But you won't be flying in a hypersonic airliner any time soon. It could take more than 20 years to build one.

The first supersonic flight was made on October 14, 1947, by US Air Force captain Chuck Yeager flying a Bell X-1 rocket plane.

Fascinating Fact

We're really moving!

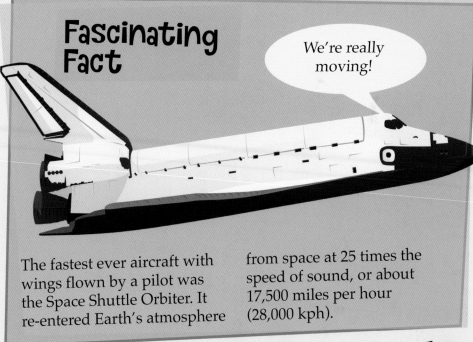

The fastest ever aircraft with wings flown by a pilot was the Space Shuttle Orbiter. It re-entered Earth's atmosphere from space at 25 times the speed of sound, or about 17,500 miles per hour (28,000 kph).

Aircraft use radio signals from a fleet of Global Positioning System (GPS) satellites in space to pinpoint their position anywhere in the world.

Steering

W hen we want to turn a corner while walking, we use the force of friction between our shoes and the ground to push us in a new direction. Pilots steer planes without anything solid to push against. They do it by using panels called control surfaces. Most planes have three types of control surfaces—ailerons in the wings, elevators in the tail, and a rudder in the tail fin. When the pilot moves the controls, the control surfaces swivel out into the air streaming past the plane. The air pushes against them and this turns the plane.

Pitch, Roll, and Yaw

Planes can move in three ways, called pitch, roll, and yaw. Pilots use all three of these movements to steer a plane in any direction.

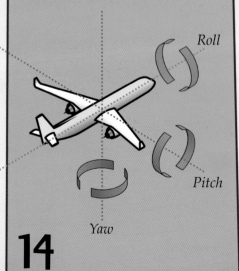

Roll

Pitch

Yaw

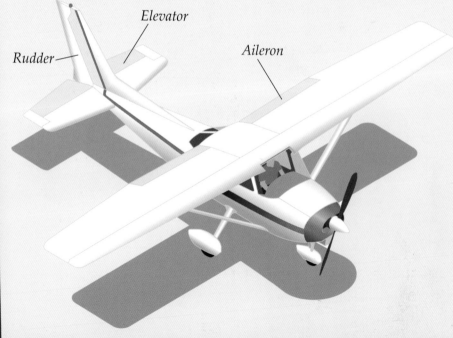

Elevator

Rudder

Aileron

14

Hands and Feet

A pilot uses both hands and both feet to steer a plane. Pulling or pushing the control column makes the plane climb or dive. Turning the yoke at the top of the column rolls the plane to one side, and pushing two foot pedals turns the plane's rudder.

Flying is a very hands-on experience!

Why It Works

Some of the latest airliners are steered by means of a small control called a sidestick. It looks like a game controller. Moving the sidestick sends signals to a computer, which then steers the plane.

When a plane turns, people inside it feel a force called g-force. The tighter and faster the turn, the greater the g-force.

Pilot Power

In a small plane, moving the controls pulls cables, which move the plane's control surfaces. In bigger, faster planes, a pilot is not strong enough to move the control surfaces by muscle power alone. Moving the controls sends electrical signals to machines called actuators that move the control surfaces.

15

Flight Instruments

Air Pressure

Air pressure falls as you go higher above the ground. Three of the six basic instruments use air pressure, or changes in air pressure, to measure a plane's altitude, speed, and vertical speed.

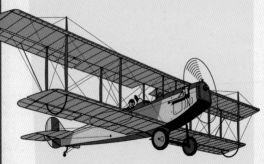

The air pressure we feel at Earth's surface is caused by the weight of all the air above pressing down on us.

An aircraft instrument panel used to be covered with lots of dials and gauges showing information about the plane and its engines. There might be dozens of them in a small plane, or hundreds in a large airliner. Today, nearly all of these instruments have been replaced by computer screens, but up to six of the old-style instruments are still used alongside the computer screens. Three of them work by air pressure and three use gyroscopes. If the computer screens fail, a pilot can still fly a plane safely by using these simple mechanical instruments.

Airspeed indicator

Altitude indicator

Altimeter

Turn indicator

Heading indicator

Vertical speed indicator

Gyroscopes

A gyroscope is a spinning wheel that resists attempts to tilt it. Three instruments use gyroscopes to show a plane's direction, whether it is flying level, and whether it is turning correctly.

Let me check my gyroscope...

Magnetism

Planes may also have a magnetic compass that uses Earth's magnetism to show the plane's heading (direction).

The magnetism that makes a compass needle turn to point North is caused by liquid iron spinning around the center of Earth.

Fascinating Fact

Some cell phones and other gadgets can now be controlled by the user talking to them. Aircraft are beginning to use this technology, too. So far, it's being used mainly by military aircraft, but pilots of all kinds of aircraft will soon be able to talk to their plane's computer.

Computer, are we there yet?

Air Launch

Experimental rocket planes are usually air-launched. They are carried into the air hanging underneath a bigger plane. At the right altitude (height), the rocket plane falls away and fires its rocket engine. Air-launching saves weight, because the rocket plane can carry less fuel.

The X-15 holds the speed record for a powered, piloted aircraft. On October 3, 1967, William J. Knight flew it to a top speed of 4,520 miles per hour (7,274 kph).

Rocket Planes

Experimental planes designed to fly very high or very fast are often powered by rocket engines instead of jet engines. Engines need oxygen to burn their fuel. In thin air at high altitudes, there is very little oxygen. So rockets carry a tank of oxygen, or a chemical that contains oxygen, as well as a tank of fuel. One of the most recent rocket planes was SpaceShipOne. It had a top speed of three times the speed of sound and made the first private manned spaceflight in history in 2004.

X-15

In the 1950s and 1960s, a top secret American rocket plane called the X-15 made dozens of flights, reaching a top speed of more than six times the speed of sound at the top of the atmosphere. Lessons learned from its flights were used in the design of the Space Shuttle.

The Bullet Plane

When the first supersonic plane, the Bell X-1, was being built, no one knew what shape a supersonic plane should be. They knew that some bullets travel faster than sound, so the Bell X-1's nose was made the same shape as a bullet.

The faster a plane flies, the hotter it becomes. Parts of the X-15 rocket plane reached a temperature of 2,400°F (1,315°C).

Fascinating Fact

X-15 pilots wore pressure suits that made them look like astronauts. Some X-15 pilots did fly so high that they left the atmosphere and went into space. A pilot becomes an astronaut if he or she reaches an altitude of 62 miles (100 km).

Long and Thin

A glider's wings are extremely long and thin. It's the best shape for producing a lot of lift but very little drag. This lets a glider fly a long way without losing much height.

Look, No Engine!

Gliders are planes without engines. Only three of the four flight forces act on a glider—lift, drag, and weight. There is no thrust. At the beginning of each flight, a glider is towed into the air behind a plane or pulled along the ground and into the air by a winch. Once a glider is flying, the pilot can go higher by flying into rising air currents. The rising air carries the glider up with it. Gliders are designed to create the most lift with the least drag, so they can stay in the air for as long as possible.

The world record for distance flown nonstop by a glider is 1,402.4 miles (2,256.9 km), set on January 12, 2010, by Klaus Ohlmann. He holds more than 30 gliding records.

Looking for Thermals

Warm air is lighter than cool air, so it floats upward. Rising currents of warm air are called thermals. Glider pilots search for a thermal and fly in tight circles to stay inside it as it carries them upward. Then they fly to the next thermal and the next.

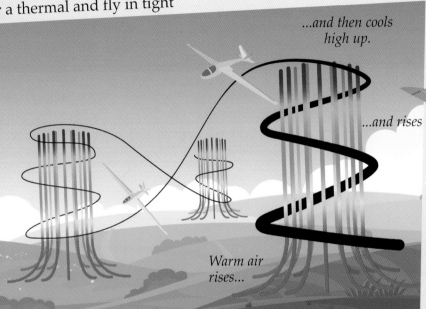

...and then cools high up.

...and rises

Warm air rises...

Hang Glider

One of the simplest flying machines is a hang glider. It's a sheet of fabric tied to a frame. The pilot hangs underneath it and controls the glider by shifting his or her body forward, backward, or to one side.

Lift divided by drag is called the lift-to-drag ratio. The higher the number, the better. It's about 18 for an airliner, and up to 70 for a glider.

Try It Yourself

When air rises in a thermal, moisture in the air forms fluffy clouds in the cold air at the top of the thermal. You can find thermals by looking for these fluffy cumulus clouds on a sunny day.

Backpack Propeller

A paramotor, or powered paraglider, is a backpack housing a small engine with a propeller. The propeller spins inside a metal cage for safety. The pilot hangs underneath a long, wing-shaped parachute.

A propeller at the front of an aircraft, pulling the aircraft along, is called a tractor propeller. A propeller at the back, pushing the aircraft, is called a pusher propeller.

The Smallest Flying Machines

Flying machines come in all shapes and sizes. Some of them are small enough to strap onto the pilot's back. Most of these small aircraft are powered by an engine driving a propeller, but some are jet-powered, and a few are even rocket-powered. Swiss pilot Yves Rossy invented a carbon fiber wing with four small jet engines. He straps it to his back, turning himself into a human jet plane that flies at up to 185 miles per hour (300 kph), using only movements of his body for steering.

Is it a bird?
Is it a plane?

Micro Flyer

Microlights and ultralights are the smallest planes. They usually have an open cockpit or seat hanging underneath a simple wing or hang glider, so these aircraft are sometimes called powered hang gliders. They're powered through the air by a propeller at the back.

Astronauts wear a jet pack during spacewalks outside the International Space Station in case they drift away from the spacecraft.

Rocket Belt

A rocket belt, or jet pack, is a backpack that uses downward-pointing jets to lift the pilot off the ground for short flights. The pilot steers by tilting the jet pipes. The gas tanks on the pilot's back contain enough fuel for flights lasting about 30 seconds.

Up, up, and away!

Why It Works

A rocket belt works by splitting a chemical called hydrogen peroxide into steam and oxygen. The hot gas expands rapidly and bursts out of two nozzles as jets, producing enough thrust to lift the pilot off the ground.

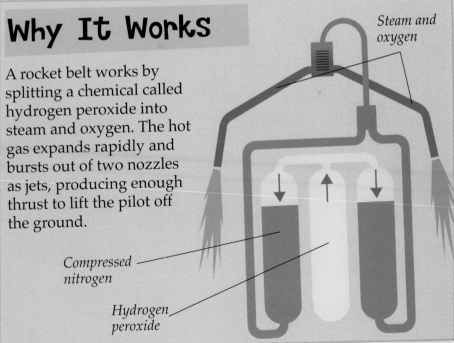

Steam and oxygen

Compressed nitrogen

Hydrogen peroxide

Helicopters create lift by spinning a set of long thin wings called blades. The spinning blades are called a rotor, and aircraft that use spinning rotor blades are called rotorcraft. Even when a helicopter stays still, its spinning blades produce lift, so helicopters can do things that most airplanes can't. They can hover in one spot in the air and even fly backward! They can also take off and land vertically, so they don't need a sprawling airport with long runways. Their unique flying abilities make them ideal for search-and-rescue work.

Stopping the Spin

When a helicopter spins its rotor blades, the blades push back and try to spin the helicopter in the opposite direction. Most helicopters stop this by having a small rotor at the end of their tail. It blows air sideways with enough force to stop the helicopter from spinning.

The first practical, modern helicopter was the Sikorsky VS-300, built by Igor Sikorsky in 1939. It was the first helicopter with one main rotor and one small tail rotor.

The Tail Rotor's Missing!

Some helicopters have a tail, but there is no rotor at the end of it. Instead, a fan blows air through the tail. It blows out of a hole on one side at the end of the tail, doing the same job as a tail rotor.

Tilt-Rotor

A tilt-rotor is a very strange-looking aircraft. Rotors at the ends of its wings spin like helicopter rotor blades to make a vertical takeoff. Then the engines and rotors tilt forward and the aircraft flies like a plane, using its wings for lift.

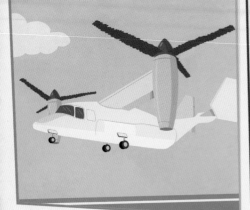

Can You Believe It?

A gyroplane flies by using a rotor that isn't driven by an engine. It freewheels. A propeller pushes the aircraft along. Air flowing through the rotor blades keep them spinning and creating lift.

Electric Aircraft

Electric motors are much smaller, lighter, and quieter than jet engines. And batteries have improved so much that they can now store enough electrical energy to power a full-size, piloted aircraft. A few electric aircraft are solar-powered. Their wings are covered with solar panels, which convert solar energy into electrical energy to power electric motors turning propellers. Most electric planes built so far have been experimental planes used for research, but practical electric planes are now being developed to carry passengers and cargo. The Airbus E-fan is an experimental two-seat electric plane.

Solar Plane

Solar Impulse 2 was the first piloted, solar-powered aircraft to fly around the world. The journey took 23 days between March 2015 and July 2016, with 16 stops. It flew on solar power during the day and batteries at night.

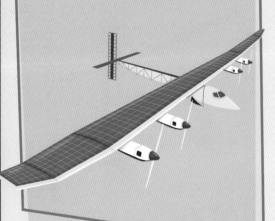

Air Taxi

The Airbus CityAirbus is a battery-powered rotorcraft being developed as an air taxi for use in cities for flights lasting up to about 15 minutes. At first, it will be flown by a pilot, but later it will fly the four passengers without a pilot onboard.

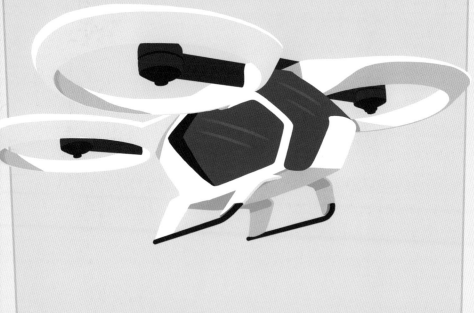

Multi-Prop

The NASA X-57 Maxwell is a battery-powered plane being developed now. It is powered by 14 electric motors driving propellers. All the motors are used for takeoff, but only the two wing-tip motors are used when the plane is cruising at about 175 miles per hour (280 kph).

The first electric aircraft was built and flown as long ago as 1883. It was an airship built by French scientist Gaston Tissandier.

Fascinating Fact

Several aircraft manufacturers are developing electric airliners. An aerospace company in Europe is working on an electric airliner called E-Thrust. It will be propelled by six battery-powered electric fans. During each flight, the batteries will be charged by a generator driven by a small jet engine.

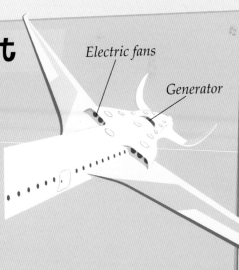

Electric fans

Generator

27

The Strangest Planes

It was not possible to build an aircraft with forward-swept wings until lightweight, stronger-than-steel materials like carbon fiber were invented.

Flying a Wing

One way to reduce the drag that slows a plane down is to make the whole plane in the shape of a wing, with no body or tail. It's called a flying wing. It's a very difficult aircraft to fly. It can be flown safely only with the help of computers.

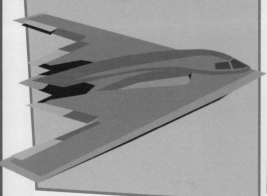

Designers and engineers are constantly trying different ways to build planes that are faster, bigger or quieter, or kinder to the environment. New types of military aircraft aim to avoid detection and to carry out their missions more successfully. Sometimes, a plane has to be designed for one particular, specialized purpose. One such plane is the Airbus A300-600ST Beluga. It was named Beluga after a type of whale. It's a giant plane with a huge cargo hold for carrying parts of airliners to factories where planes are built.

Wrong Way Around

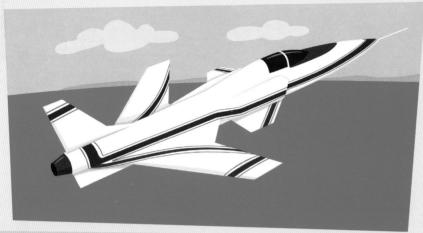

An experimental plane called the X-29 looks as if its wings have been attached backward. They're called forward-swept wings. Two of these aircraft were built and flown by NASA and the US Air Force, and it turns out that backward-facing wings work very well.

Sea Monster

A giant jet plane nicknamed the Caspian Sea Monster was designed to fly over water at a height of less than 33 feet (10 m). It was supported by a cushion of air trapped under its wings as it flew along. The huge aircraft was powered by ten jet engines—eight at the front and two more in its tail.

The first super-size transport plane was the Aero Spacelines Pregnant Guppy, built in the 1960s to carry parts of giant rockets for the US Apollo space program.

Why It Works

The cavernous cargo bay of the Airbus Beluga can carry items up to 124 feet (37.7 m) long and weighing up to 47 tons. This is possible because the whole front of the aircraft above the cockpit opens up for cargo loading.

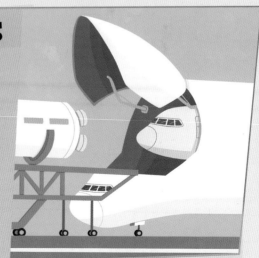

Glossary

Aileron A hinged panel in a wing that makes a plane roll to one side.

Airfoil A device with curved surfaces designed to create lift when it moves through air.

Airplane A heavier-than-air flying machine with fixed wings.

Air pressure A force acting on a surface because of the weight of air above.

Altitude The height of an aircraft above the ground or sea level.

Cargo Goods carried by an aircraft or other vehicle.

Cockpit The part of an aircraft where the pilot sits.

Control column A lever in a plane's cockpit that is moved to steer the plane.

Control surface Part of an aircraft, such as the rudder, aileron, or elevator, that is moved to steer the aircraft.

Delta wing A triangular wing.

Drag A force that resists the motion of an object such as an aircraft through air.

Elevator An airplane control surface that raises or lowers the tail.

Energy The ability to do work.

Flap A device fitted to a wing to produce more lift for flying safely at lower speeds during takeoff and landing.

G-force A force produced by acceleration.

Glider An aircraft designed to fly without engine power.

GPS The Global Positioning System, a fleet of 24 navigation satellites in orbit around Earth.

Gravity The force that attracts everything toward the center of Earth or toward any other object.

Gyroscope A spinning wheel or

disk that resists attempts to tilt it.

Hydrogen peroxide A chemical compound containing hydrogen and oxygen, similar to water but with more oxygen.

Hypersonic Faster than five times the speed of sound.

Lift An upward force produced by a wing as it moves through air.

Microlight A very small aircraft.

NASA National Aeronautics and Space Administration, the US government space agency.

Oxygen A gas that forms about one-fifth of Earth's atmosphere.

Paramotor A motorized, steerable parachute.

Piston engine A type of engine with disks moving back and forth inside cylinders.

Pitch One of the three ways in which an aircraft can move, by tilting its nose up or down.

Pressure suit Protective clothing worn by the crews of very high-flying aircraft and spacecraft.

Propeller A device with two or more blades that spin to move an aircraft or boat.

Rocket A vehicle propelled by one or more rocket engines by burning fuel with oxygen, both of which are carried inside the rocket.

Thrust A pushing force that propels (moves) a vehicle.

Winch A towing or lifting device made of a rope or cable wound around a motorized drum.

Index